# DAUGHTER, WHY DO YOU WORRY?

# Daughter, Why Do You Worry?

## Sever Ties from Emotional Strongholds and Live Your Best Blessed Life!

### Keishana A. Crenshaw

XULON PRESS

Xulon Press
2301 Lucien Way #415
Maitland, FL 32751
407.339.4217
www.xulonpress.com

Unless otherwise indicated, Scripture quotations taken from the King James Version (KJV) – *public domain.*

Scripture quotations taken from the Holy Bible, New Living Translation (NLT). Copyright ©1996, 2004, 2007 by Tyndale House Foundation. Used by permission of Tyndale House Publishers, Inc.

Scripture quotations taken from the Amplified Bible (AMP). Copyright © 1954, 1958, 1962, 1964, 1965, 1987 by The Lockman Foundation. Used by permission. All rights reserved.

Scripture quotations taken from the English Standard Version (ESV). Copyright © 2001 by Crossway, a publishing ministry of Good News Publishers. Used by permission. All rights reserved.

Paperback ISBN-13: 978-1-66286-380-6
Ebook ISBN-13: 978-1-66286-381-3

# INTRODUCTION

Many people place a lot of pressure on themselves to attain the picture-perfect life. Our parents or grandparents coached some of us on how to be a good spouse, parent to your children, and member of society. This wisdom is valuable beyond measure, but sometimes it accompanies an expectation that places pressure on us to achieve a certain standard. Where does this standard come from? We are often gauging goals and accomplishments by the world's standards. We want approval and want to feel valued and appreciated. Don't most human beings? What is it that presses us to compete with ourselves and one another? What is the cost as it relates to our peace and happiness?

We worry and suffer from self-doubt, depression, and anxiety. We fight to attain the status quo of what society considers success. Some never come to the realization that the void we are trying to fill in life can only be accomplished by being in the center of God's will, not by the things we attain or life accomplishments.

In this book, I will share the process God brought me through to identify my *why* in every area of my life. "Why" is probably the most important question you will ever ask yourself! The key is seeking and obtaining God's purpose for each season and every area of your life.

We get lost in society's expectations, and our focus shifts from divine purpose to selfish purpose. I have observed men and women lose focus; they lost sight of the dream and forgot their why. Years later, they are astonished by the fact that their children have animosity against them. We parents will sometimes push our children to do what we want them to do because we didn't fulfill our purpose. We place demands on them to pursue a particular career or interest because we are trying to live our lives through them. Unfulfilled purpose leaves a void that never goes away.

Can I share something with you? Your purpose is not something your great brilliant mind created. It came from God the Father. You, my friend, were wonderfully made to do the spectacular, achieve greatness, and represent excellence, which all glorifies God the Father, creator of all things! Yes!

Let me give you a little background before you delve into the meat of this book. On November 8, 2021, I took my first step of blind faith when I announced to my employer of nineteen years that I planned to retire from the company. You may ask, what's so special about that? People retire from their jobs all the time! Well, I'm forty-eight years old with no investments, savings, retirement funds, or arrangements to fall back on. Sounds crazy right? What would possibly make someone choose to walk away from their career and main source of income?

Let me take you back a couple of years to the summer of 2019. This was the year I suffered a heart attack while on a lengthy conference call at work. The intensive care unit team called me a miracle! I say they are exactly right! But this wasn't the first time God had worked a miracle in my life, and He's not done with me yet.

During my time of healing, I spent a lot of alone time with God; sitting, listening, meditating on God's Holy Scripture . . . being still! In my stillness, God began to speak to me about my next season and the plans He has for me, which will *shift* me into something new, something different. I didn't know His full plan, but He began speaking to me about writing.

Over the years, I had different websites where I blogged and wrote daily affirmations. This wasn't the direction He was taking me. God told me to begin writing books using the experiences I have gained from ministry, life, and being a board-certified life coach.

One day while taking in some sun in my backyard and hanging out with my teenage sons, they began to ask me about when I planned on being purposeful and using my God-given gifts to help people. Wow, what a revelation! Out of the mouth of babes! They began to explain that I've been so peaceful and less stressed since I was home resting from the heart event. They said helping people brings me such joy, and everyone can see it. I guess everyone but me . . . They took notice that when I minister or coach a person or family, I'm in my zone, and they can see that this is what I truly enjoy, not the corporate life I had become accustomed to. Don't get me wrong; my job was awesome. I had a great team, supportive peers, and the company I represented took care of their employees well. In my mind, I had it all and planned to work until I was at a ripe old age.

The conversation with my sons led me to ask the question, what's my why? I will discuss this in the coming chapters. As a result, I decided to seek God for direction and clarity. God was speaking clearly, but for a year, I disobeyed God's directive. I wanted to be comfortable, I wanted job security, and I wanted the stability of a guaranteed pay check every two weeks! Within that year, my emotions began to change. I wasn't enjoying my job anymore, but there was no reason for me to feel this way. There was a shift. This spiritual shift began affecting me in the natural. I was being drawn away from what made me comfortable.

During this period, I began receiving the desire of God's purpose for me to begin writing, making myself available to help others, and going deeper in the ministry He called me into. I now had to align with the will of God for my life because it had become such a desire that I didn't want to do anything else. My convictions were so dominant that I had to repent for delaying for so long. I submitted to God and confessed that I would trust Him because He is the one who has brought me this far as we have history and an intimate relationship that has been tried and proven over and over again.

My future is not in my hands, and my provision does not come from my job. It is God who brings provision through various avenues, and if He has called me to step into a deeper level of faith, it is because He wants to bring me into a deeper level of testimony! Can I get an amen? Listen to me, my dear reader. I want to share the processes God took me through to bring me to a greater level of trust, worship, and complete surrender. God wants to get the best out of you. He does this by putting *His* best into you. This is done by walking through every journey, every trial—life! God wants His children to live their very best, blessed life.

I trust that this book will bless you beyond measure.

# ABOUT THE AUTHOR

Keishana Angelic Whittingham was born on January 13, 1974, to Keith Leroy Whittingham of Kingston, Jamaica and Sharonann Lynette Ingham-Whittingham of Paget, Bermuda.

Keishana graduated from Bloom Township High School in 1992, served in the United States Navy as a signalman, and later obtained a bachelor of science degree in telecommunications management from DeVry University in 1999.

On June 27, 2003, Keishana married Wesley Howard Crenshaw of Benton Harbor, Michigan. Wesley and Keishana have three children together: Kayvon, Jaydon, and Rylen. The family currently resides in the state of Illinois. Wesley and Keishana are known to be a power couple in ministry. They work together within the marriage ministry as well as various entrepreneurial endeavors.

Keishana has been a Board-Certified Coach™ since 2011. She received her training through The Coaching and Leadership Institute in Forest Park, Illinois, mentored by CEO Dr. Derrick Johnson LCPC. In addition,

Keishana holds specialty certifications in Divorce Transitioning, Work-Life Balance, and Wellness.

Keishana and Wesley are both ordained and licensed ministers since 2012. Keishana serves in the governmental office of prophetess, and Wesley is the associate pastor at Worldwide Deliverance Ministries, Inc. in Plano, Illinois, under the leadership of Apostles Michael and Lynette King where they have been faithful members since 2007.

As a coach and minister, Keishana is passionate for people. She often ministers by her various testimonies of victoriously overcoming depression, anxiety, hurt, abandonment, physical and sexual abuse, rejection, and low self-esteem. Serving in a deliverance ministry, Keishana is unwavering in her conviction that God can deliver anyone from the strongholds of satan, should they desire to be free. Keishana strongly believes in the free gift of salvation, the power of the Holy Spirit, the power of prayer, and the powerful Word of God!

# ACKNOWLEDGMENTS

I first acknowledge God my Father for His gift of salvation through His Son, Jesus the Christ. I thank my heavenly Father for the gifts He has placed upon my life and anointing and appointing me as a light bearer for His kingdom. I thank God for the opportunity to author books that will inspire and produce greatness that will cause every reader to press harder and go further to live their best, blessed life. It is an honor to share my testimonies and wisdom I have attained through the Holy Spirit to encourage, guide and be a living epistle to others.

To my beloved husband, Wesley. I thank you for truly being the covering God ordained. You unceasingly pray for me and have encouraged me in the night seasons. You've ministered to me in love and correction and have been my tree of Lebanon that never broke or wavered, even in the most difficult of times. The level of faith you have shown has consistently been an arm of strength to bring me up to greater levels of faith and to pursue a deeper, mature relationship with God. Thank you for allowing God to use you in immeasurable ways. I love you.

To my children. Each of you is truly the fruit of God's favor! I am so blessed to be chosen by God to experience motherhood and be a witness to your physical and spiritual birth, growth, and development. God has blessed the Crenshaw Five to be a five-fold ministry within our own house. You have each ministered to me and shown such great spiritual wisdom during the process of my journey, which is just beginning. I am super excited to see what God does with each of you next. Thank you for obeying God above all else and committing yourselves to a lifetime of service as kingdom ambassadors!

Kayvon, keep preaching the gospel! You have such a passion for the lost and the heart of a shepherd to teach with patience and commit to those who have been rejected and experienced church hurt. God has shown you His love, and others are drawn to you by that same love that shines through you. Surely, miracles, signs, and wonders will follow you as you follow God!

Jaydon, keep interceding by your powerful prayer life and allowing your light to shine through the kindness you show to everyone. You are truly a prophet of God, a dreamer, and a mighty man of valor. Soar, my son! You are quite the storm; never settle for anything less than greatness!

Rylen, stay in God's presence! As a worshiper, God is revealing the secret things to you through His Spirit. Never allow the fear of the unknown to hold you back in your worship. God is definitely eager to bring you into the deep and into places many Christians aren't willing to go. Dive deep, my son! No limits!

My pastors, who are also my spiritual parents, beloved friends, and apostolic covering, Michael and Lynette King. My life has been forever changed from the moment God sent me into the Lakewood Springs Clubhouse to attend Wednesday night Bible study. I thank God for the two of you! Thank you for loving me amid my brokenness. I thank you for having a heart after God above everything else. I've never seen either of you waver from the Word of God. Both have been an example that this walk can be lived as nothing is impossible with God. You showed me that God doesn't want me to be perfect; He just wants my obedience and complete surrender. I never knew the realness of God's character until I learned about intimacy with God. This is just the beginning, and I am overcome with an expectation of what God is doing with this ministry in the years to come! I love you both.

Lastly, I must include a special acknowledgment to the apostle I met in Florida in the summer of 2021. I don't recall his name, but if you are reading this book, I thank you for your obedience in allowing God to use you in a spectacular way! God gave you the unwavering boldness to approach two strangers in the grocery store and prophetically release into our spirits for over two hours! My God! My spirit still leaps within me when I think of that day. One of the things God gave you that has impacted my life forever is when you looked into my eyes and said, "Daughter, why do you worry?!" No one but God knew the internal struggles I was fighting, and those five words broke me to a place of complete surrender and began my journey in discovering my why's.

The process that followed birthed this book, which was prophesized as well. I thank God for you, man of God! I pray our paths cross again.

# DEDICATION

I dedicate my first published book to my late father Leroy Keith Whittingham (2002), and my mother, Sharonann Lynette Ingham (2022). I thank God for the life lessons obtained from both of my parents. I am not a preacher's kid, nor was I raised in the church. My life was quite the opposite! My parents loved to party; they were alcohol and drug users. I spent lots of time in bars and night clubs, even falling asleep in the club manager's back office. My father ran numbers in the 1970s and was a restaurateur, and my mother was a barmaid at night and worked as a nurse during the day. We were a middle-class family living in the suburbs of the Midwest in the 1980s.

My parents had a very passionate marriage. When they loved one another, they loved hard! But when they didn't get along, the relationship was extremely violent! I observed many things within the course of their nine-year marriage, which laid the foundation to the paths I would take in my teenage and young adult years. I don't share this to shed a negative light on either of my parents. They lived a life separated from God in those years, so the expectation of making bad choices, living unhealthy lifestyles, and those associated repercussions is what comes with that side of the walk. When satan rules your life, you must expect a life of disastrous events marked by great loss, lasting distress, suffering, and hardship.

You may ask why I am thankful for this upbringing. It was through my sufferings and traumatic experiences that I obtained the anointing on my life! There is a cost, my friend, but I thank God for it because God used it to cultivate my ministry and develop the person I am today!

Later in life, both of my parents developed a personal relationship with God. Our relationships were mended, we were healed and forgiven of past hurts, and God blessed us immensely! Over the course of my life, my parents were a vital piece of my growth as a Christian woman. The enemy did not want me to be born! He's made many attempts to destroy me and kill my destiny! God said not so! I thank God for who He chose to bring me into this world. My parents were not perfect, and neither am I. The awesome thing is that God doesn't want our perfection; He just wants our heart!

If you were here today to read this, I'd say thank you, Dad and Mom, for being your genuine selves. You did your best for where you were in life within various seasons of your lives. Most of all, I thank you for loving me! Until we embrace again in glory!

Your daughter,
Keishana (Keishie aka Baby Girl)

# WHY DO YOU WORRY?

Worry, fear, doubt, and anxiety were emotions I struggled and fought against throughout my childhood, teenage, young adult, and adult life. They were always present in one way or another despite where I was in life; good times, milestones, achievements . . . worry, fear, doubt, and anxiety were always there embedded in my mind, even in my soul. I couldn't understand why I just couldn't be happy and stay happy or at least content with myself and my life. Do you ever feel this way? No matter the circumstance or where you are in life, worry shows up with its cousins: fear and doubt. God granted me the opportunity to write this book to share my experiences and continual journey on the battlefield of the spirit realm against the demonic strongholds whose assignment is to tear down and destroy! Destroy what? The God-designed purposes for your life! God intricately made each of us uniquely destined for greatness. Certainly, God of the universe and all creation would not place limitations on the things He desires to see accomplished through us.

Romans 8:28 (KJV) states, "And we know that all things work together for good to them that love God, to them who are the called according to his *purpose*" (emphasis mine).

Jeremiah 29:11–13 (NLT) states, "For I know the plans I have for you," says the Lord. "They are plans for good and not for disaster, to give you a future and a hope. In those days when you pray, I will listen. If you look for me wholeheartedly, you will find me."

Wow! How awesome is that! I get so excited when I read God's Word. Why? Because I know it to be true. How? I've tried God at His Word many, many times, and guess what? It's never failed! So, let's go back and start with the building blocks of what it means to be a called. In Christianity, believers are appointed (called) by the Most High God.

2 Timothy 1:9 (ESV) states, "Who saved us and called us to a *holy calling*, not because of our works but because of his own purpose and grace, which he gave us in Christ Jesus before the ages began" (emphasis mine).

1 Corinthians 7:17 (ESV) states, "Only let each person lead the life that the Lord has assigned to him, and to which God has called him."

What does it mean to have a calling on your life? It means you have purpose! As children, many of us had aspirations to achieve or be a part of something we measured as great. Do you ever wonder where that desire came from? Yes, parents and other adult figures play a part in molding those ambitions, but the seed came from God. We just read that God has *given* to us our purpose. What we often see in life is that we lose sight of those purposes because we allow other *things* to take priority in our lives instead of keeping God's will as priority. We get married, and our spouses' needs become priority, education and career goals become priority, children's needs become priority, and finances become priority. Sometimes we have to put our wants aside because we have to take care of an ill parent. Well, you say, isn't this just life? We have to accommodate and re-evaluate what we consider as priority as circumstances change, don't we? Absolutely not, when we are in God's will for our lives, His Word tells us that He provides for every need. Glory to God!

Philippians 4:19 (ESV) states, "And my God **will** *supply every need* of yours according to his riches in glory in Christ Jesus" (emphasis mine).

Many know the popular prayer from Psalm 23:1 (ESV), "The Lord is my shepherd; I shall not want." This is a promise to those who trust in and rely on God as their source. We must believe in the God of creation and know without a doubt that His Word is truth.

As we proceed in this book, I will provide the scriptural tools on how to accomplish this. For now, let's continue digging into purpose. Purpose, by definition, according to Webster 1828 Dictionary [1](Webster 1828, Purpose definition & meaning 2022) states, that which a person sets before himself as an object to be reached or accomplished; the end or aim to which the view is directed in any plan, measure or exertion. One Greek translation of purpose is boúlēma (boo'-lay-mah) and defined as a pre-set, fully-resolved plan. I love this! Let's have a Selah moment here and absorb the depth of this definition." A pre-set fully resolved plan"! Pre-set, already in place, resolved. You didn't have to DO anything to arrange it. It's already done! There is no figuring out strategies or plans to the process. God already took care of all if it. You just need to trust God and walk in the process that will take you into your purpose! We are predestined for greatness in God because it's been His plan from the very beginning. Walk with me on this!

I'm sure we all know of someone who is a parent of adult children who has strained relationships because they've never allowed their children to live out their own purposes. They've tried to influence every decision when it comes to athletics or any extracurricular activity to degree major and career planning to bring into fruition the things they have never fulfilled. Now, most parents never intend for their actions to cause harm to their children, but they are subconsciously not living in their purpose, and the desire is to still see it accomplished. As a result, these adult children are resentful because they weren't allowed to make their own choices.

There is a spiritual void because we are not in the purpose of what God has for us. You say, "I want the voids in my life filled. I want my life to be purpose-driven! How do I attain this?" Well, I must first ask, have you obtained salvation through Christ Jesus. If not, it is essential we begin with how to obtain salvation because the scriptural promises are only for those who are believers.

What is salvation? According to Romans 10:8–11 (AMPC):

> But what does it say? The Word (God's message in Christ) is near you, on your lips and in your heart; that is, the Word (the message,

the basis and object) of faith which we preach, Because if you acknowledge and confess with your lips that Jesus is Lord and in your heart believe (adhere to, trust in, and rely on the truth) that God raised Him from the dead, you will be saved. For with the heart a person believes (adheres to, trusts in, and relies on Christ) and so is justified (declared righteous, acceptable to God), and with the mouth he confesses (declares openly and speaks out freely his faith) and confirms [his] salvation. The Scripture says, No man who believes in Him [who adheres to, relies on, and trusts in Him] will [ever] be put to shame or be disappointed.

Isn't this just amazing? You don't need to fix yourself for God to accept you. He doesn't want your perfection; He just wants your heart! Many of us strive or drive toward the approval or affection of other people. You don't have to attempt to impress God with your accolades or how good of a person you are. God knows us better than we know ourselves and despite it all—the good, the bad, and the ugly.

Once you obtain salvation, all the promises in God's Word are available to you. You only need to believe God, trust God, and rely on God, Adhere to God's instructions in His Word. He won't disappoint! We let one another down all the time, but not God; it's not in His nature.

1 Peter 5:10 (ESV) states, "And after you have suffered a little while, the God of all grace, who has called you

to his eternal glory in Christ, *will himself restore, confirm, strengthen, and establish you*" (emphasis mine).

This is another promise to the believer. Life is filled with various challenges, and there are processes we must walk through as part of our growth and maturity as a believer, a child of the living God. These challenges sometimes accompany seasons of suffering. The glorious thing about having a personal relationship with the Father is HIS PROMISES. One of them is the measure of faith the believer is given to allow them to endure the difficult times.

Many of us often seek for someone or something to take away the pain, loneliness, hurt, betrayal, unforgiveness, shame, bitterness, and emptiness. Some try to fill these voids through sexual lust, alcohol, drugs, self-mutilation, and other toxic avenues. But as we just read, when we surrender ourselves to God, He himself will restore us to His plan, will strengthen us, and establish us through Christ Jesus. This is God's grace, my friend. Our history doesn't matter; what does matter is HIS-story! We have everything we need in Jesus. God is so awesome! Following salvation is the gift of the Holy Spirit.

Acts 2:38 (ESV) tells us, "And Peter said to them, 'Repent and be baptized every one of you in the name of Jesus Christ for the forgiveness of your sins, and you will receive the gift of the Holy Spirit.'"

As you begin to seek after God, you will begin to receive revelation, guidance, and instruction by His Holy Spirit. In seeking the Lord, you will begin to learn of Him, His character, and His will; this is how you receive revelation of your purpose. The seed of His purpose is in you. It's been there from before you were developed in your mother's womb.

God told the prophet Jeremiah in Jeremiah 1:5 (AMPC), "Before I formed you in the womb I knew you, and before you were born, I consecrated you; I appointed you a prophet to the nations."

Jeremiah 29:11–13 (AMPC) states, "For I know the thoughts and plans that I have for you, says the Lord, thoughts and plans for welfare and peace and not for evil, to give you hope in your final outcome. Then you will call upon Me, and you will come and pray to Me, and I will hear and heed you. Then you will seek Me, inquire for, and require Me [**as a vital necessity**] and find Me when you search for Me with all your heart."

These Scriptures carry a wealth of information. I first want you to understand that God provided us with these historical accounts of various individuals' lives to show us that they are no different than you and me today. We are presented with similar circumstances and are told to trust in and rely on God. We see this repeatedly in God's Word. Jeremiah was called, Abraham was called, Mary was called, and so were you! I challenge you to read the above referenced Scriptures in Jeremiah aloud as affirmations. Make it personal!

Hebrews 4:12 (AMPC) tells us, "For the Word that God speaks is alive and full of power [making it active, operative, energizing, and effective]; it is sharper than any two-edged sword, penetrating to the dividing line of the breath of life (soul) and [the immortal] spirit, and of joints and marrow [of the deepest parts of our nature], exposing and sifting and analyzing and judging the very thoughts and purposes of the heart."

Selah moment! Please reread Hebrews 4:12. Read it in different translations; for example, The Message or English Standard Versions. Then, allow the Holy Spirit to really break it down to you. When we read and speak Scripture, it begins to manifest in our lives. It first begins as a seed that's planted in our spirit. We desire the Word; it becomes food to our spirit, and we crave it. The Word then begins to stir a transformation within our lives.

Romans 2:12 (NLT) says, "Don't copy the behavior and customs of this world, but let God transform you into a new person by changing the way you think. Then you will learn to know *God's will for you*, which is good and pleasing and perfect" (emphasis mine).

If God's will for us is pleasing and perfect, then why would we want to live in our own purpose away from God? Why do we choose to live in worry, fear, and doubt? Because we have not obtained understanding.

Proverbs 4:5 (AMPC) tells us, "Get skillful and godly Wisdom, get understanding (discernment, comprehension, and interpretation); do not forget and do not turn back from the words of my mouth."

What's the first step in obtaining understanding? The first is to respect God. This is the "fear of the Lord" referenced in Proverbs 1:7a (ESV), "The fear of the Lord is the beginning of knowledge." We must know that the Holy Spirit, through Christ Jesus, gives understanding.

1 John 5:20 (ESV) says, "And we know that the Son of God has come and has given us understanding, so that we may know him who is true; and we are in him

who is true, in his Son Jesus Christ. He is the true God and eternal life."

Next is study, study, study God's Word. You will never have a successful relationship in the natural if you don't spend quality time together in order to become acquainted with one another. It's the same principle when it comes to learning of God and becoming acquainted with him personally to know His personality, heart, likes, and dislikes—His will.

What is the purpose of Scripture? 2 Timothy 3:16–17 (ESV) tells us, "All Scripture is breathed out by God and profitable for teaching, for reproof, for correction, and for training in righteousness, that the man of God may be competent, equipped for every good work."

Now, let us draw the line in the sand regarding the Bible. We've heard what critics say about the Bible; they question its authenticity and many other attributes of God's Word. I believe in the simplicity of facts, not to overstate or overthink things. I just believe God. If His Word tells me that Scripture is the breathed logos (word) of God. Then I believe it! I believe everything in Scripture is truth. I believe the Holy Spirit breathed into mankind the Word of God, written into text for the believer. It is our instruction manual for living life in the earth realm. Fun fact: B.I.B.L.E. is an acronym for Basic Instructions Before Leaving Earth.

I have provided you with the starter tools for accepting Jesus as Lord of your life to obtain salvation and the purpose of studying God's Word. This is the foundation on which living a life of purpose is derived. As you begin to build from this basis, you will gain spiritual understanding of who you are in God. To be freed from worry, doubt, and anxiety, you must go back to the beginning to gain an understanding of who you are in God, who God says you are! We must learn our true identity.

For many of us who have lived by the society-driven standards of the world, we have accepted the labels given to us. Can I let you in on something you may not know? You've been hoodwinked, my friend! Yes, at one time, we all believed the lie before the truth was revealed to us. The prince of the air spiritually governs the "world." Who is that? satan! Yes, satan caused you to forget who you are and your *real* identity in the kingdom of God, causing us to live a life of rebellion against God's will for our lives.

Ephesians 2:2 (AMPC) tells us, "In which at one time you walked [habitually]. You were following the course and fashion of this world [were under the sway of the tendency of this present age], following the prince of the power of the air. [You were obedient to and under the control of] the [demon] spirit that still constantly works in the sons of disobedience [the careless, the rebellious, and the unbelieving, who go against the purposes of God]."

Today I decree the scales that satan has placed over your eyes will fall away, and you will learn of your identity as an ambassador of the kingdom of God! An heir with Jesus Christ! Today you will see yourself in your true position, a position of authority!

In Genesis 1:26–28 (KJV), we read:

> And God said, Let us make man in our image, after our likeness: and let them have dominion over the fish of the sea, and over the fowl of the air, and over the cattle, and over all the earth, and over every creeping thing that creepeth upon the earth. So God created man in his own image, in the image of God created he him; male and female created he them. And God blessed them, and God said unto them, Be fruitful, and multiply, and replenish the earth, and subdue it: and have dominion over the fish of the sea, and over the fowl of the air, and over every living thing that moveth upon the earth.

The first point here is understanding that we were made in God's image, after His likeness. Wow! Can you grasp the gravity of this proclamation? God is spirit, so He gave us His spirit! It's been gifted to us. We only have to receive it. Say, "Father, I receive your Spirit in Jesus's name. Wasn't that easy? You may ask, "I don't feel any different. Was something supposed to happen?" Trust me; something happened, but it was internal.

As you develop maturity in your relationship with God, you will learn that those five senses of your body (flesh) will no longer govern you. You will no longer operate by *feelings*, physical or emotional. You will learn by simply trusting God at His Word; it's been accomplished. First Corinthians 3:16 (ESV) states, "Do you not know that you are God's temple and that God's Spirit dwells in you?" Romans 8:9 (ESV) tells us, "You, however, are not in the flesh but in the Spirit, if in fact the Spirit of God dwells in you. Anyone who does not have the Spirit of Christ does not belong to him."

What is His likeness? In Galatians 5, we learn of God's "fruit," meaning His character, some of which include love, patience, peace, faithfulness, joy, goodness, gentleness, humility, and self-control. We must understand this is part of our DNA, our human makeup. With the Spirit of God residing inside of us, the seeds of His character germinates and produces fruit, which is seen externally in our character. The Bible tells us we are able to identify the spirit of a person by their fruit.

Next, we were given dominion, territory over the earth, and every living thing in the earth. Whoa! How is that factual? Because God said it! We are commanded to subdue the earth. Another word for subdue is *calm*. Why is the earth so tumultuous if we are told to maintain serenity and peace? Well, the master manipulator, father of lies, aka satan, came in and brought the curse of sin. But sin didn't negate our position on earth and the authority we have. How is that, you ask? Jesus! Our Savior and Redeemer! Jesus outplayed satan in his own game. Next thing you know . . . checkmate! Jesus put us back into our original intended position from Genesis 1! God loves us SO much that He already had a plan. That devil thought he had everything figured out . . . But God!

So, I ask, who are you?

First Peter 2:9 (AMPC) tells us, "But you are a chosen race, a royal priesthood, a dedicated nation, [God's] own purchased, special people, that you may set forth the wonderful deeds and display the virtues and perfections of Him Who called you out of darkness into His marvelous light."

Yes, God said it, and that seals it. So be it! Fear and doubt will make you believe you are unworthy of this calling of royalty, but I tell you the truth: satan is a liar. The Bible tells us in John 8:44 (ESV), "You are of your father the devil, and your will is to do your father's desires. He was a murderer from the beginning, and *does not stand in the truth, because there is no truth in him*" (emphasis mine). When he lies, he speaks out of his own character, for he is a liar and the father of lies.

Satan only has three tricks he has attempted to use to fool mankind. They are the lust of the eye, lust of the flesh, and the pride of life. How so, you ask? He uses the eye to make you look at yourself in the natural; your limitations, your downfalls, and he calls you unworthy of this calling. Remember, God says in First Peter 2:9, we are a new creation in Christ Jesus, His chosen ones, a royal priesthood, a holy nation! But his opinion of you doesn't matter. All that matters is who God calls you!

Next, satan uses the flesh; our weaknesses, sin, judgment, senses, emotions, and faithlessness.

Lastly is the pride of life. "What will people say?" You look and sound foolish. A royal priesthood? Really? You can't pay your bills, you're a horrible parent, your children hate you, you're no good to anyone, you have no authority, no one respects you, and you're weak, uneducated, and useless!

Again, why does satan do this? To bring confusion and cause you to doubt who you are and the authority you carry!

Hey, if satan hasn't used this on you, he's certainly used it on me on many occasions. His whole goal is to have you shift your eyes from God and close your ears to God's voice. How does he do that? Through discouragement and doubt, he will press and press until you can't bring yourself to read God's Word. You lose faith and sight of who you are! Once he's done that, his job is done.

We do a great job of picking up from where satan left off. He only needs to plant the seed of rejection, bitterness, and unworthiness, and we begin to agree with him; we begin to speak the opposite of what God's Word says about us.

Let me share a bit about my past. I was what some would call an introvert, very shy and quiet. I avoided large groups of people if at all possible. Why? Because at a very early age, I accepted satan's lie that I was unwanted, strange, a freak, and weird. I then adapted the persona of what I thought to be true of myself. I thought I was weird, so I displayed weird characteristics, which made people stay away from me. This was satan's way of separating me from people so he could inflict spirits of depression upon me.

My childhood was very, very dark. You see, I didn't know a thing about God as a child, but He was always present. How do I know? Because I'm still here! God may not have stopped the afflictions, but He used them to build my character and the person I am today. What satan meant for evil, God our Father turned it for my good! I had to be deprogrammed. I needed to obtain the mind of Christ to see myself as God the Father sees me. He had to take away my heart of stone, which caused me not to like people or myself, and He gave me a new heart.

He shows me daily what real love looks like. I tell you, this believer's walk of faith will make all things new in your life if you would only allow God into your life, heart, and mind so that He can make all things new for you, just as He's done for billions of believers around the earth!

Proverbs 18:21 (ESV) says, "Death and life are in the power of the tongue, and those who love it will eat its fruits."

We must be mindful of what we speak. The Word of God tells us to put our hands over our mouths when we are tempted to speak foolishly! Proverbs is also lovingly known as the book of wisdom; chapter 8 specifically provides the reader of wisdom's character and origin. I suggest studying the entire book as it provides a wealth of information on how we are to conduct ourselves. I consider these proverbs excellent golden nuggets for life as it addresses many of life situations.

We must take a stand against satan and be aware of his tricks so we are not caught off guard. You must unequivocally know who you are in God! satan will play on your emotions and even use life circumstances to bring doubt. God's Word tells us to stand; we must be firm and unwavering. Trust me; you will get there, and once you do, satan better run quickly because once you grasp the authority you carry, nothing, and I mean absolutely nothing, will be able to shake you from God's will for your life. On the other hand, YOU will be the one doing the shaking! Shaking down satan's kingdom, that is! Ha!

It gets even deeper. You're God's spokesperson on earth! Yep.

Jeremiah 15:19 (AMPC) states:

> Therefore, thus says the LORD [to Jeremiah], "If you repent [and give up this mistaken attitude of despair and self-pity], then I will restore you [to a state of inner peace] So that you may stand before Me [as My obedient representative]; And if you separate the precious from the worthless [examining yourself and cleansing your heart from unwarranted doubt concerning My faithfulness], You will become My spokesman. Let the people turn to you [and learn to value My values]."

The first step is repentance from our stinking thinking. The deceiver, satan, distorted our thinking and created a fake reality in which most of us believed prior to us receiving the knowledge of Christ Jesus; therefore, removing the veil of deception. We repent for our ignorance in choosing the lie over truth. With repentance comes restoration! This is why I tell you that God is so awesome. We don't have to beg for forgiveness over and over again. If it's real, and you'll know if it's real or not. How? Conviction—sin will grieve you; you won't desire to continue in your former ways. You will desire truth and renewal. God restores us back to our intended position on earth and relationship with Him. Remember Genesis 1? We must align ourselves in God's Word.

As His representatives, we are to reflect the kingdom in which we are ambassadors. This is evident in our character, what we speak, our actions, and our demeaner. It is no different than a government ambassador. When an ambassador goes to another country, they are representing their country of origin; everything they do and speak is a reflection of that country. They operate under the authority bestowed to them by their country.

In Genesis 1, we were given authority over the earth. God says we are ambassadors of the kingdom of heaven. We are a royal priesthood. Read 1 Peter 2:9 and 2 Corinthians 5:11–21. If God says it in His Word, why do we allow those under satan's influence to identify us otherwise? From this moment forward, I challenge you to only respond to who God says you are. When you begin to operate in your authority, your countenance and everything about you will change as you clothe yourself in your royal garments and the mind of Christ Jesus.

I consider it such an honor to share the gospel of Jesus, to teach and be taught, to hear and receive, and to love and be loved. God is love, and there is nothing that surpasses that!

My friend, you don't have to remain stuck in the cycle of the world system. There is liberty in God! The Word of God tells us that *nothing is impossible with God* (Luke 1:37). Remember earlier how I shared that worry is a cousin of doubt and fear. If we root our belief in the fact that *we can do ALL things through Christ who strengthens us,* we leave no room for fear and doubt to enter our minds or hearts. We worry because we are not grounded in Christ Jesus.

Romans 11:36 (AMPC) states, "For from Him and through Him and to Him are all things. [For all things originate with Him and come from Him; all things live through Him, and all things center in and tend to consummate and to end in Him.] To Him be glory forever! Amen (so be it)."

Did you catch that? All things begin and end in God. My friend, we all need a *so be it* attitude. If you've been purposed to do something, you need to trust God completely that He has a plan and path for you to take that will lead you into the fulfillment of your calling no matter the obstacles, closed doors, and naysayers. Despite the process, we must say, "So be it" because we know that it must come to pass!

This book's purpose is to bring daughters and sons into the understanding that you don't have to settle. You can dream big! Attain the unimaginable! Allow God to plant the seeds of purpose!

First Corinthians 2:9 (KJV) tells us, "But as it is written, Eye hath not seen, nor ear heard, neither have entered into the heart of man, the things which God hath prepared for them that love him."

In my years of work/life balance coaching, I've met so many individuals who came into our first session feeling defeated and doubtful that change could happen for them. They've spent most of their lives surviving, doing what needs to be done to provide the essentials for their families. We find ourselves becoming weary of the constant cycle between work and home. If we're honest with ourselves, many of us aren't really living!

In 2021, I decided that every day for the remainder of my years, I would live my best, blessed life. I actually made it my motto! Why? After forty-seven years of life, I knew that this couldn't be it. I knew I hadn't reached my potential. I realized that I had so much more in me that I hadn't even begun to discover. As I was teaching others how to balance work and personal life as well as how to tap into those inner goals, I was learning; the greatest teachers must first be practical learners!

This is the gleaning process. I'd rather learn how to get out of the ditch from someone who's been in the ditch. They can be compassionate and understand my perspective rather than the individual who wants to give advice from the position of looking down into your situation! I've climbed out of my share of trenches in life. My purpose is to assist you in identifying your "why" in life, which will bring you into the even bigger revelation of living your best blessed life!

In the introduction of this book, I shared my process of receiving my purpose of becoming an author as well as some of the challenges I faced. Fear and doubt showed up immediately. I've always depended on a "9 to 5 job" as my source. I started boot camp a week after graduating high school. After serving in the Navy, I worked while attending college . . . I've always worked. I never knew the fundamentals of trusting God as my source when it came to a paycheck because I always had one!

It's usually when one is placed in a position of not having an income that they learn firsthand the true meaning of God's provision. When I heard the voice of the Lord tell me that it was time to leave my job of nineteen years to write full-time, I was shaken to the core! I considered myself to be a woman of faith. I had history with God; He had brought me into a relationship with him and walked me through the process of overcoming depression, anxiety, rejection, fear, and anger. But this thing right here! Oh! My Lord! I was truly at a place where I had to be still to receive the instruction of what God desired to do with me.

This involved separation, fasting, and sitting before God in His Word. Why? I had to silence my flesh. What does that mean? I was encompassed with fear and doubt. These spirits are not of God. God wanted me to know Him as my source of a provider. I've known Him in various other areas of my life, but this was next level. He wanted me to trust him completely. This is what I affectionately call tenacious faith! I had to stay focused and push myself to stay grounded in studying God's Word daily so I could hear his voice. The fact that God wanted to activate a part of me that had not yet been tapped into, satan immediately came with his demonic influences to cause me to delay or cancel God's purpose for this season of my life.

When the flesh comes against the spirit of God, you have to silence it! We all have experienced satan's attacks, but we've never properly identified it as spiritual warfare. Too often, we shake it off and say we have bad luck or things we plan to do never work in our favor. Today is your wake-up call! I speak to your spirit and command a shaking and stirring to drive you into your purpose! I decree and declare over your life that you are unstoppable as you press toward your seeking in the Lord. You will not only discover your purpose for this season of your life, but you will also continue to be a powerhouse for the kingdom of God and bring glory to God in all that you do in the mighty name of Jesus!

You've been under attack by the enemy's camp because God has a plan and purpose for your life. satan will send every sort of distraction to destroy and tear you down so that you never realize who you are and to whom you belong! Our hearts must be turned toward God, and our one desire should be to love and please him through our obedience. YES, obedience! It's not a well-liked word because it makes many feel as if they are being forced into servitude, a position where they need to "obey."

Many people were raised under an iron fist and forced into obedience through harsh discipline. As adults, they have worked to attain a particular stature in life where they are in charge, and no one will tell them otherwise! I get it. But this is the type of thinking we adapted from society and world structure.

Remember, you are a new person in Christ Jesus. Along with that, we have to attain a new mindset. As an ambassador representing the kingdom of heaven, we now follow the statues as provided within God's Word. God's Word says in John 15:14 (KJV), "If you love me, you will keep my commandments." Now that's real talk! How can you say you love God and appreciate all He has done in your life BUT continue to do what *you* want to do?! Well, doesn't God accept me just as I am? When you first come to Him, absolutely, yes! God doesn't expect for you to fix yourself because you can't. In fact, you'll probably mess yourself up even more. Let God have His perfect work in you in His timing and through His process.

When I came to God, I was a hot mess! I continued in my sin while attending Tuesday and Wednesday night Bible studies, Thursday night prayer, Sunday school, and worship service. I was hungry for God but not yet transformed. I was in an unholy relationship, living a life of sexual immorality, perversion, lying, blasphemy, cursing, partying in demonic clubs, and drinking their fruits. I was still producing fruit of the devil because that's the only life I knew.

As I continued to submit to God, He began to take those desires away. Part of your salvation is surrender, a surrendering of your will, ways, and ideologies. In return, God makes all things new, but remember, it's a process. God expects those who are called by His name to be obedient to His Word. There is no grey area here. God calls disobedience witchcraft. You are not His and cannot call yourself a Christian if your life doesn't align with the Word of God. To live a life apart from God makes them sons of disobedience.

Titus 1:6 (ESV) says, "They profess to know God, but they deny him by their works. They are detestable, disobedient, unfit for any good work."

Catch this! God says they deny him by their works. Your lifestyle should bear the fruit of God's Word. If you still reflect the world, then God is not in you. God gives us the authority to judge the fruit of the congregation. His Word tells us we will know one another by our fruit. Don't be fooled; there are many spirits in the church. These are individuals with various demonic strongholds that have yet to be set free by the Holy Spirit.

Mark 1:21–26 (ESV) says:

> And they went into Capernaum, and immediately on the Sabbath he entered the synagogue and was teaching. And they were astonished at his teaching, for he taught them as one who had authority, and not as the scribes. And immediately there was in their synagogue a man with an unclean spirit. And he cried out, "What have you to do with us, Jesus of Nazareth? Have you come to destroy us? I know who you are—the Holy One of God." But Jesus rebuked him, saying, "Be silent, and come out of him!" And the unclean spirit, convulsing him and crying out with a loud voice, came out of him.

Don't judge yourself by what you see others doing. The enemy has agents even sitting in the pews of the most holy sanctified churches. These demonic agents are there to bring disorder to the house of God by using individuals to bring mischief, gossip, deceit, spread doubt, and impart disbelief and discouragement. We are, however, to judge ourselves according to God's

Word. If you are walking through the process of deliverance so you can be freed from the demonic strongholds that bound you when you were separated from God, you have an opportunity to change things again through your surrender, giving your disobedience to God, and open yourself to the Holy Spirit so that He can reposition you to where you should be in God. This walk isn't rocket science, my friend, but God gave us everything we need in His Word. Read it, meditate on it, study it, pray it, and allow His Holy Spirit to have His perfect work in you!

This is the only way to avert satan's snares. When God was speaking to me about His plan for this new season in my life, I began to question him. I said, "Lord, how will we make it financially? I have a mortgage, debt, three young adults in college, and no savings!"

God responded immediately! He said, "OH! So, your job is your source? I thought all provision comes from me?"

I said, "Well, yes, all provision does come from you, but you have always brought provision through dependable jobs."

He responded, "So are you saying that I can only work through the world's system? I thought I was God of all creation. All things exist because I allow it. Is nothing impossible for me? If I called you to accomplish something, why don't you trust that my plan includes meeting your every need? Am I a God of lack or insufficiency? No! I am the God of more than enough, I am the God of multiplicity, and I am a God of purpose and order!"

I was truly humbled by this dialogue with God and was repentant for doubting the dominion, authority, and lordship of God over my life.

I gave God my yes! I submitted my concerns and asked that He would strengthen me through it and show me how to be immovable and unwavering in my trust in His plan. It's all about surrender, my friend. Blind faith means that you will undoubtedly trust in and rely on God's plan and process no matter the circumstances. You must be tenacious in your conviction of faith! This means to take your eyes off of your bank account, limitations, ability, education, skillset, and anything where you are the primary contributor! Why? It's not about you. It's about God being glorified through you!

I think we need a selah break here so you can fully digest the magnitude of what you just read.

The Bible tells us in 1 Corinthians 10:31b that whatever we do, do all to the glory of God. It's all about shifting our thinking from the natural to the biblical. What do I mean? Let me break down the difference between a natural way of thinking and biblical thinking. The world system throughout history has been compiled of various influences that include but is not limited to demographic and ethnic backgrounds, religion, social order, economics, morals, and tradition.

We acclimate to those system influences, which become part of our state of being, our character. For example, we may hear people say, "I have this tendency because it's my family culture" or "I've never learned of God for myself; I've always practiced the religion I was taught by my family. It's tradition that my family is and always will be Pentecostal; it's all we know." This is a learned behavior attributed to what we see and hear during our upbringing.

The same application above can be used for biblical thinking. *It's a learned behavior.* If a child is taught to live by biblical doctrine and sees it by the lifestyle of their parents, they adapt this form of thinking and character. Some are not raised with biblical thinking, so it must be learned. We must retrain our way of thinking. How is this done?

Romans 12:2 (NLT) tells us, "Don't copy the behavior and customs of this world, but let God transform you into a new person by changing the way you think. Then you will learn to know God's will for you, which is good and pleasing and perfect."

Study God's Word, my friend; spend time with God in prayer. As you spend time with the Father, you will be transformed by His spirit. It's amazing! You'll never want to go back to your old way of thinking once you have the mind of Christ.

I recall trying to quit smoking cigarettes in my twenties. I tried various cessation methods like medication, gum, and patches. I may have stopped for a brief time and would pick up the habit again. When I gave my heart to God, my only desire was to please him. I still had a lot of junk in me along with my natural ways. I was still drinking, smoking, cursing, sinning . . . all of it. This is why His Word tells us to come as we are. We can't fix ourselves; we fail repeatedly. But when we come into relationship with God, He does the changing.

At a mid-week prayer service, I went to the altar and asked God to remove anything in me that grieved Him. That night, I left the altar delivered! God is so awesome and loving that he took away my cigarette addiction. I didn't have the craving to smoke, no withdrawal symptoms, or mood swings. I just stopped, and the smell actually became a horrible stench to me, so I was never tempted to go back when being in the company of other smokers. That, my friend, was God! I never looked back.

The more of myself I gave away, the more complete I became in God. That is not to say there weren't any struggles. Yes, at times, this flesh of mine put up a good fight, but my spirit was willing to allow God to do whatever He wanted to do in me for the perfecting of my faith and the building of my character. The struggle between ourselves (flesh) and the spirit is real, my friend.

The test began immediately when God spoke to me about this new season. My husband and pastors had confirmed God's Word, and now was the time to step out and let faith take action.

In November 2021, I notified my employer that I would be leaving the company to pursue my calling of becoming an author. I provided the company with five months to allot time to put things in order for my transition. Remember, God establishes order and always has a process. I could not simply provide a two-week notice and bounce. I had a key position within the company, and we needed sufficient time to transition responsibilities, perform training, and set details in order. I had to adhere to God's process as this was His directive.

1 Corinthians 2:9 (ESV) says, "But, as it is written, 'What no eye has seen, nor ear heard, nor the heart of man imagined, what God has prepared for those who love him.'"

I heard this Scripture over and over in my spirit. God was telling me that He wanted to bless me immensely. I just had to stay the course and trust God.

In April 2022, I retired from *my work* and began *His work*! Was I nervous? Absolutely! But fear was not my portion, and I would not allow it to take root in my mind. This was God's plan, and I trust that according to Ephesians 3:20, He is able to do exceedingly, abundantly above all I could ever ask or think according to His riches in glory! So, here we are. I sit here today writing this book to encourage you to step into your God-given purpose for this season of your life. God is limitless! That means there is nothing you can't achieve if God has called you to accomplish it. We just need to trust God in the process and know that everything we need, He *WILL* supply.

You may say, "That's great for you, Keishana, but I don't have that type of relationship with God. I'm not where you are." You don't have to be where I am. Our journeys are different, and your God-designed path was made specifically for you. Just like your fingerprint, it can't be duplicated. We are all carpenters; we have the same tools and are trained how to utilize them by the same teacher (the Holy Spirit). The path to creating your masterpiece is your own! Enjoy the process, learn from it, and continue to grow! First things first, take the step. To do so, let's look into where you are currently in life.

# WHERE ARE YOU?

G enesis 3:9 (KJV) says, "Then the LORD God called to Adam and said to him, 'Where are you?'"

This wasn't a question of Adam's geographic location. God asked this of Adam because their connection was broken by sin. Their covering (connection with God) was removed, and they were exposed (sin), revealing their nakedness. Remember earlier we read that God created Adam in His image and likeness. Adam and Eve lived in the garden of Eden.

Genesis 2:25 (NLT) tells us, "Now the man and his wife were both naked, but they felt no shame."

Why did they not feel shame? Embarrassment, indignity, and humiliation were not of God's character. They were spiritually *covered*, shielded, and protected by the Spirit of God. satan's temptation brought in sin, which removed God's covering, leading to a separation from God.

As a result, we see Adam's response to God in Genesis 3:10 (NLT), "He replied, 'I heard you walking in the garden, so I hid. I was afraid because I was naked.'"

I ask you today. Where are you?

Isaiah 59:1–2 (ESV) states, "Behold, the Lord's hand is not shortened, that it cannot save, or his ear dull, that it cannot hear; but your iniquities have made a separation between you and your God, and your sins have hidden his face from you so that he does not hear."

Have you felt the tugging of the Holy Spirit drawing you to God, but the separation seems so great that you can't get to where you need to be? We all have felt this, and that's a good thing! That means we have hope. God has not counted you out. Aren't you glad God isn't fickle like people? We are sometimes quick to discard the people in our lives.

In this chapter, I'd like you to perform some self-evaluating. It's all about discovery! We sometimes need to look at where we are in our lives. Are we in purpose? Are we living our best, blessed lives?

Ponder this: what is God speaking to you at this moment?

When I first heard God speak to me about this new season He was taking me into, I had to consider these very same questions. As we mature in the Christian faith, we go from "faith to faith, glory to glory." We each have various assignments we are given as we remain steadfast in the center of God's will for our lives. I knew for some time that God was elevating me spiritually, and I was expecting a shift but didn't know where that change would lead. As I began to look at my spiritual gifts and skillsets, I thought, *How can they be used to further the gospel and glorify God? Is there something new God is desiring to move me into, or is it something I've been doing that I need to dedicate more of my time and effort into?* God will use people or situations to provide an answer or confirmation to the things you ponder in your heart.

One day, my middle son asked if I had ever considered writing to share my experiences as a life coach, ministry, and personal testimonies to help others. He continued to state that he noticed I had a peace about myself when I did something to help others.

My excitement when I'm performing this type of work is very evident. They can see it makes me happy.

My sons were so encouraging to me during this discussion. They gave me the bump I needed to begin seeking God even further for direction toward my next steps. Soon thereafter, I began receiving prophetic confirmations through God's servants He also began to show me intricate details in my dreams of this next season. He showed me that I would be participating in seminars, speaking engagements, prayer lines, and implementing a prophetic ministry as an extension of our home church. Was I completely blown away? Absolutely! Shocked? Not at all. We serve a great God! I knew if I was being elevated spiritually, then God would also manifest a promotion in the natural as well.

"So," you say, "I'm not where you are, Keishana. My faith isn't there to trust God and step into the unknown. Please do not compare your life experiences to mine."

I use transparency in coaching and ministry to show people that it's possible . . . all of it! I didn't wake up a mature Christian. It took many, many years. For most of those years, I was very disobedient to the Word of God. I was what the Bible would call a lukewarm Christian. This is one who straddles the fence per se. I wanted to do my own thing but had the expectation to receive the full benefits of a believer without conversion. You know the saying: you can come on my front porch, Jesus, but you're not invited into my house.

We want to control when and how we allow God into our lives, but God wants all of us. He expects a complete surrender of our hearts. I can completely understand that! Who likes to be cheated on No one! It doesn't feel good to give your heart to someone who isn't willing to reciprocate that commitment. As my pastor often reminds our congregation, it's a love affair! God wants an intimate relationship with us, meaning He wants all of us for Himself! He doesn't want to share you, nor should He. God loves us so much that He gave! Yes, He gave it all, and He's still giving every moment we breathe the breath of life. The surrendering of oneself is your sacrifice. Are you willing to lay it all down and say, "God, have your way in me?"

After years of kicking rocks and asking God why my feet were always sore and bloody, I had to identify the obvious. Stop kicking rocks! We often do more damage to ourselves pushing against God instead of just following Him. Unfortunately, we can be stubborn people. We sometimes have to be so broken or just tired of being tired to even consider allowing God to take over. But you know what? If that's what it takes, then so be it.

The path will vary for each of us, and I want you to arrive at the destination of living your best, blessed life! Can you look at where you are today and say, "I may not be where God wants me to be, but I'm willing to do what is necessary to get there"? Or you may be in a transition as I am. You're stepping out into something different; some may say even a bit crazy, non-traditional, but if you look at the lives of every innovator, their dream was crazy for their day!

Think about it, flying . . . how absurd! I even think of the historical account of Noah in the Bible. The people had never seen or heard of rain. What's that? (Remember, in those times, God watered the earth from the ground. Water never came from the sky prior to the flood! Read Genesis chapters 6–8.) "Why are you building this enormous boat?" The people of Noah's day thought he was a lunatic. Do you see where I'm going with this? Don't count it out because it appears strange; you don't know if your family will support you or if people will shun you. Walking away from a secure career seemed crazy! People who didn't know how to trust God as their provider would say, "How will you pay bills, eat, and maintain the necessities of life?"

It's not for me to figure out. My job is to receive the plan and walk out the process! How easy is that? I spent years working long hours, which was mentally and sometimes physically stressful. I would receive a project from my boss and would have to put together the process of how to get it done, set a timeline for implementation and completion, and get the work done! No excuses; we get the job done so we can get that paycheck, don't we? Well, with God, he already has the plan and the process! We only need to hear His instruction and do the work.

James 2:14–18 (AMPC) tells us:

What is the benefit, my fellow believers, if someone claims to have faith but has no [good] works [as evidence]? Can that [kind of] faith save him? [No, a mere claim of faith is not sufficient—genuine faith produces good works.] If a brother or sister is without [adequate] clothing and lacks [enough] food for each day, and one of you says to them, "Go in peace [with my blessing], [keep] warm and feed yourselves," but he does not give them the necessities for the body, what good does that do? So too, faith, if it does not have works [to back it up], is by itself dead [inoperative and ineffective]. But someone may say, "You [claim to] have faith and I have [good] works; show me your [alleged] faith without the works [if you can], and I will show you my faith by my works [that is, by what I do]."

Selah moment! Reread the Scripture and meditate on it. It's time to eat the whole roll of this Word.

It's about taking action! When evaluating where you are in this current season of life, you must peel away the layers of the external forces that keep us from hearing God. Trusting God's plan is one thing; we can trust and believe in anything, but if we never act on it, we never grant ourselves the opportunity to make it real. It's all about going to the next level. None of us stayed in first grade for our entire childhood and then one day became an adult. There is a progression in life that we must walk through that touches every area of our mental and physical development.

My husband always shares this example in his ministry lessons. When our sons were babies, they would sometimes knock things from the table onto the floor because they didn't know any better. If our sons, now teenagers, are still knocking items from the table onto the floor as a child, then we as parents may need to look into obtaining professional help.

This next level requires us to search ourselves, to really dig deep into life as we currently know it. Where do you find happiness? Do you find yourself living life through others, such as your children? Do you find yourself constantly trying to escape your current reality through things? I recall being into fantasy or science fiction books as a teenager. Why? I could escape my reality in the books I had read.

I was very lonely being raised as my mother's only child. I was what one would call an introvert. I wanted to have friends and be popular, but I was very uncomfortable around people. I was very quiet and shy. Truthfully, I just didn't trust people. When I was around my peers, I found myself constantly lying. I felt that my life was boring and of no interest. So, when people would actually talk to me, I sometimes gave them a fake name and would create a world I wanted them to know. God forbid if people actually learned that I was a rejected teen whose mother abandoned her and had experienced sexual and physical abuse as a child. I was an emotional wreck! Many, many years as an adult had passed before

I was able to come to terms with my reality and choose to acknowledge it to heal.

In this process of self-discovery, we sometimes need to dig things up that we have buried to be our very best selves. This, my friend, is the purpose of this book. Worry, fear, and doubt can be rooted in various life events. From my earliest memory, I recall always carrying a spirit of worry and fear. I had anxiety whenever I left home because in my mind, the world wanted to harm me. I didn't trust anyone because I was being abused. It seemed anywhere we went, I was never safe. Can you imagine how this type of mindset could plant the seed for emotional trauma? This seed of negativity began to stretch its roots into every area of my life as I became older.

During my process of self-discovery, I had to go to the graveyard and dig out those circumstances from my past. No, it isn't pleasant. I'd say acknowledging my past and learning to forgive others as well as myself was the most difficult process I've ever walked through and probably ever will. If you are at a point in your life where you are tired of being controlled by your past circum-stances, then I challenge you to allow God to guide you through the process of acknowledgment, healing, and discovery of the real you. Allow yourself to receive help from others as well, whether it be your pastor, prayer partner, coach, therapist, or any mixture thereof. We often tend to think of the word *help* as a bad four-letter word. This is just another deception of satan.

Isaiah 41:10 (ESV) states, "Fear not, for I am with you; be not dismayed, for I am your God; I will strengthen you, I will *help* you, I will uphold you with my righteous right hand" (emphasis mine).

As you seek direction to identify where you are, know that God is with you all the way! We don't need to fear the process; God's got you! I know firsthand how fear can paralyze you from moving forward in your purpose. I experienced various traumatic events in my youth, and as a result, I found it difficult as a teenager and young adult to recollect many of the day-to-day details of my childhood. This is identified as dissociative amnesia It's the mind's way of protecting itself from these experiences.

The key is to continue to allow the Holy Spirit to work through the process. Just because you are a work in process, doesn't mean you can't be in purpose, that you can't accomplish many great things in life. It's just the opposite! you are a constant work in progress, you are doing amazing things and can be in the center of God's will for your life if you allow Him to lead you. The act of submitting ourselves to the Holy Spirit allows for transformation.

Ephesians 4:22–24 (AMPC) tells us:

> Strip yourselves of your former nature [put off and discard your old unrenewed self] which characterized your previous manner of life and becomes corrupt through lusts and desires that spring from delusion; And be constantly renewed in the spirit of your mind [having a fresh mental and spiritual attitude], And put on the new nature (the

regenerate self) created in God's image, [Godlike] in true righteousness and holiness.

Whoa. Isn't this fantastic? We don't need to be stuck.

God talks about stagnation in His Word. He discourages it. Keep on moving, keep on pressing, and keep on allowing yourself to be open to receive all that God has for you. Always remember that it's a process we define as "a natural phenomenon marked by gradual changes that lead toward a particular result." ([2] Merriam Webster, Process definition & meaning 2022)

Have you ever heard the adage, "Rome wasn't built in a day"? Gradual is the key word here. I know in our desperation to make something happen, we want immediate results. But we must realize anything of worth or value takes time to develop. The refiner's fire has to be extremely hot to melt gold. During this process to obtain a result of pure gold, dross must be removed from the liquid gold. This dross carries various types of impurities, such as other metals, minerals, and dirt. Once this content is extracted, we see the final product, which is absolutely beautiful for the eye to see, and we pay much more for pure gold as well. Ha! I hope you caught that!

We must allow the Holy Spirit to refine us daily. He is pouring into us His character, His heart, His qualities, and His love! As He pours into us, He draws out that dross, the hidden sin that we don't discuss with anyone. Even thinking about some of the things we've done brings us shame. But the Bible tells us in Micah 7:19b (ESV), "You will cast all our sins into the depths of the sea." And Hebrews 10:17 (ESV) tells us, "I will remember their sins and their lawless deeds no more."

Our Father is a God of impossibilities! When we can't forgive, God forgives. He throws our sin into the depths of the sea so He will remember them no more. I personally think this is just phenomenal! We often beat ourselves up mentally and prevent progress in our lives because of unforgiveness. We don't go beyond our hurt and disappointment. Even when it comes to forgiving ourselves for our past mistakes, we put up walls that hinder us from being our best selves.

During this process of self-discovery in learning who we are in God, what He says about us, and where we are in this moment in time, we will see it's by His love alone that gives us what we need when we need it.

In most cases, people don't invest time into something or someone they don't care about as time is our most precious commodity. But God is not governed by time, He created time, and since He existed before time, He is patient with us. So, don't beat yourself up if it's taken you forty years to discover who you are. What's important is that you arrive!

Oftentimes, many of us have defined ourselves by our occupation, achievements, marital status, and so forth, but when we arrive at the realization that these things aren't what define us, we then begin to seek who God says we are in Him. Let's look at Scripture.

1 Peter 2:9 (AMPC) says, "But you are a *chosen* race, a *royal priesthood*, a *dedicated nation*, [God's] own [a]purchased, special people, that you may set forth the wonderful deeds and display the virtues and perfections of

Him Who called you out of darkness into His marvelous light" (emphasis mine).

Ephesians 2:10 (AMPC) says, "For we are His workmanship [His own master work, a work of art], created in Christ Jesus [reborn from above—spiritually transformed, renewed, ready to be used] for good works, which God prepared [for us] beforehand [taking paths which He set], so that we would walk in them [living the good life which He prearranged and made ready for us]."

First John 3:1–2 (ESV) says, "See what kind of love the Father has given to us, that we should be called children of God; and so we are. The reason why the world does not know us is that it did not know him. Beloved, we are God's children now, and what we will be has not yet appeared; but we know that when he appears we shall be like him, because we shall see him as he is."

Second Corinthians 5:17 (ESV) says, "Therefore, if anyone is in Christ, he is a new creation. The old has passed away; behold, the new has come."

The Word of God is life-transforming if you obtain understanding and are willing to accept its contents as truth! Let's look a little deeper into these Scriptures. First Peter 2:9 told us that you have been CHOSEN! The fact that you are this far into the book solidifies the fact that God has been drawing you to Him.

Next, He says that you are ROYALTY! Yep, that's right! God reigns over all, and His kingdom is higher than all worldly kingdoms; this makes us royalty. When you accept God into your heart, you become "reborn" spiritually. Father God then puts you on track for the purpose and plan He had for your life before you were even formed in the womb. Wow! First John 3:1–2 tells us that we SHALL be like Him.

Remember earlier in this book when we looked at Genesis, which revealed to us that we were originally formed in God's image and likeness? But then there was the fall of mankind. The awesome thing is that Jesus restored us to our original place in God through salvation. We are clothed in the righteousness of Jesus Christ. This means that He stood between man and sin so that although we are a fallen people, God only *sees* His Son. Whoo-wee! That's redemption, my friend. No one else could have paid the price for sin but Jesus! Because He did, we can now obtain all that God had intended for us from the beginning. Second Corinthians 5:17 puts the nail in the coffin! All things are NEW!

The enemy, satan, will try to convince you that this is a lie, that you are unforgivable, unlovable, and unredeemable. I promise you; he is the father of lies. You have been given a clean slate! Glory to God! Yes, indeed, ALL THINGS ARE NEW! Receive the joy of the Lord today and be still in the fact that you are loved and worth everything Jesus endured because He said so!

Whether you acknowledge God as creator of the universe and all things in it or not doesn't mean it's not fact. How do I know? Because God said it! He is King of kings and Lord of lords! We affectionately call Him Yahweh, Elohim, El Shaddai (God Almighty), Jehovah-Jireh (God our Provider), Jehovah-Nissi (God our Refuge), Jehovah-Tsidkenu (God our Righteousness), Jehovah-Shalom (God our Peace), Jehovah-Shammah (God ever present with us), Jehovah-Rapha (God our Healer), and Jehovah-Rohi (God our Shepherd)! My God! I get excited with the names of God because it identifies His sovereignty. We must acknowledge and respect the sovereignty of God!

We respect vice presidents and CEOs as well as government officials. When a judge enters a courtroom, all in attendance are instructed to stand as a sign of honor and respect. If we can give honor and respect to humans with the understanding that we are but dust who will eventually return to the ground in which we came, how can we not give much more honor and respect to the God of all creation?!

I am passionate about this because I have come to understand that I can do nothing without God. I understand who He is in position to who I am in Him. My heart melts with gratitude and humility.

I consider it a tragedy that there are "Christians" who don't acknowledge and respect God's sovereignty. They treat God like a birthday cake; they only acknowledge Him when they "feel" like it, which is, in most cases, when they need something. After God shows His hand and works things out for their good, they place Him back into the bakery box and put Him on a shelf until they "need" Him again. What an atrocity!

The *believer* should acknowledge and respect God's sovereignty because of WHO HE IS. He deserves it! Let's look at some Scriptures on the sovereignty of God.

First Chronicles 29:11–12 (AMPC) says, "Yours, O Lord, is the greatness and the power and the glory and the victory and the majesty, for all that is in the heavens and the earth is Yours; Yours is the kingdom, O Lord, and Yours it is to be exalted as Head over all. Both riches and honor come from You, and You reign over all. In Your hands are power and might; in Your hands it is to make great and to give strength to all."

Romans 11:36 (ESV) says, "For from him and through him and to him are all things. To him be glory forever. Amen."

Colossians 1:16 (ESV) says, "For by him all things were created, in heaven and on earth, visible and invisible, whether thrones or dominions or rulers or authorities—all things were created through him and for him."

Isaiah 46:9–10 (ESV) says, "Remember the former things of old; for I am God, and there is no other; I am God, and there is none like me, declaring the end from the beginning and from ancient times things not yet done, saying, 'My counsel shall stand, and I will accomplish all my purpose.'"

These are just a few examples from the Word of God that tell us who we are in Him and His sovereignty. I hope these Scriptures draw you to learn more of who you are in God and begin searching His Word for yourself.

I love topical reference guides; they provide Scripture by a specific topic. If you are dealing with anger or confusion, the topical Bible will provide all related Scripture to those key words. You can even utilize the world wide web, the Word of God, at your fingertips! Nowadays, we really don't have an excuse to not read and study God's Word as there are so many resources available to provide teaching, daily devotionals, and study methods, as well as various translations that make reading the Bible easier to understand.

Now that we have exposed satan's plan to attack the mind and the emotions that bring worry, doubt, and fear, we have uncovered the truth that you are royalty and beloved by God and have been given all authority over satan and his minions, as well as the fact that God has many and great purposes for your life! Lastly, we asked the question to ponder: where are in relationship with God? Where are you regarding your purpose in this season of your life? Are you living your best, blessed life? Do you know who you REALLY are? In this next section, we will walk through the process of finding your why. Let's go!

# WHAT'S YOUR WHY?

It's important to get to the root of identifying your why and its source. This is what solidifies our drive. When we start moving toward our purpose, various obstacles and challenges will arise. Your why will keep you focused and immovable! What else is beneficial for knowing and understanding your why? When worry, fear, and doubt rear their heads, you can crush their necks with your feet because you are walking in your divine purpose, and nothing—no devil—can change what God has prepared for you!

Can I share my heart with you today? My friend, your why will enable you to tap into the deepest part of your soul so that you can establish important fundamentals that will drive you to activate and pursue your purposes in life! To do this, we must believe in the unseen, trust for the impossible, and stand in the realm of never-ending possibilities.

Anxiety and worry have been my companions for much of my life. As a result, I've battled with high blood pressure, migraines, and heart disease for over twenty years! The enemy failed to kill me as a teenager when he oppressed me with depression. So, he brought affliction in my body. My condition baffled my primary care physician because I didn't carry the traits that come with heart disease. It wasn't in my family lineage, and I wasn't overweight, but what I did have was stress and lots of it! I was a baggage carrier.

God drew me to His never-failing love in 2004, and I became a believer. I was hungry for God! I attended church services three to four times a week. Have you ever heard the term, spinning your wheels but going nowhere? Yep, that was me. I desired God and was busy sitting in services looking for His glory to just fall on me and make everything in my life right! But I hadn't committed to change. I hadn't surrendered my ways, my thoughts, how I identified myself, and what I deemed as important.

Although I was "saved," meaning set free from captivity of sin through Jesus Christ and the fate of eternal death, I was still functioning as a worldly person who *attended* church. What do I mean by "worldly"? It's a mindset. Those who think they are their own gods don't need instruction from any supernatural force to dictate what they should do and how it should be done. They can acknowledge their belief in a supreme God who *watches* from the heavens, "but please don't interfere with my plans!" I just wanted God to fix things, but I didn't want to change, nor did I feel the need for change, although I had all these issues . . . what was I thinking?!

I needed God to do an inner work with me. It was a process. As the Holy Spirit began to teach me through His Word, I obtained understanding that God wanted a relationship with me, and the more time I spent with Him in prayer and studying His Word, the lifestyle became less about me and my wants but what God was desiring to do through me. This didn't happen overnight, my friend. I still had to deal with life and its daily circumstances, which is why I still continued to carry anxiety and worry for many, many years.

In July 2019, I suffered a heart attack while at work. During my time in intensive care, the hospital staff tried to convince my husband that he needed to prepare for the worst. This is when I witnessed the holy anointing of God come upon my husband in a way I had never seen before. There was a boldness that sprung up within him, and my husband began to decree and declare the Word of God over my body. He did this for three days! (Remember Lazarus?) My husband didn't go home to shower or sleep. Every time I opened my eyes, I would see him pacing the floor, yelling at the enemy to release this stronghold, and speaking healing to manifest in my body! He didn't contact family because he refused to prepare for a funeral.

After the third day, all of the afflictions that were in my body left. The doctors couldn't understand how I was gravely ill one day and symptom-free the next! Can I can a praise break right here?! This testimony deserves a shout! God gets ALL of the glory, my friend!

During my recovery, the Holy Spirit began to speak to me about my *why*. Why did I do the things that I did? Why did I choose to be a baggage carrier? Why did I drive myself so hard? What was purpose, truly? What did purpose mean to me? Were the ambitions that drove me completely self-seeking? Was God in it? Have I ever asked God what His will was for me? Was I in the center of His will? Was I really ready for change? Was I truly committed to following God's purpose for my life at all costs, even if it took me out of my comfort zone and familiar territory? This is when my journey to discovering my why began.

My seeking of the Lord shifted from my wants to God's heart. My prayer life changed from *I need* to, "God, what do *you* desire to for me to pray? What is on *your* heart? How can I serve the kingdom of God today? How can I be used to glorify the Father?" Then Father God began to speak to me about His will for me . . . my why.

I learned that I had to be emptied out. The answer to my why was Jesus! He is the why. This changed my entire perspective of life, career, family, finances, and ministry. Many of us come to Jesus because we are broken, are in need of a savior, and have been searching for fulfillment in our lives but found nothing but empty vessels.

Although my life changed for the better when I received salvation and became a believer, I had not matured in my thinking and understanding of God's character. I was still trying to do things my way, on my own, and for my selfish ambitions. My goals had nothing to do with my relationship with God or how my gifts and talents could be used for the ministry. Once I understood my why, my life changed! I'll never go back to my former ways of doing things. My life was solely sold out to Jesus and His purposes for me.

I strongly urge you to take a Selah moment (pause) and begin to ask yourself the same questions I referenced earlier. Write them down along with your answers.

Then seek of the Lord and ask Him these same questions; write down the answers the Holy Spirit provides. Be still, meditate on what God is saying, and ask Him to prepare your heart to receive His instruction.

Now, let's dig into purpose a bit now that we've explored our why.

I love to use agriculture as my illustrations for identifying roots and their purpose. You know who else used agriculture in their parables? Jesus! Your why is built upon the foundation of Jesus Christ. We identified earlier that God had a plan for you before you were conceived. Jesus opened the door for us to commune with God to hear His voice and learn His will for us. First Corinthians 3:11 (ESV) tells us, "For no one can lay a foundation other than that which is laid, which is Jesus Christ." The seed of God's Word is sown into us by reading and hearing.

We attend biblically grounded churches, seminars, and Bible study meetings to be poured into by those anointed to teach God's Word. In our private time, we sit quietly and meditate on the things we've been taught and study God's Word for ourselves, rightly dividing it by the leading of the Holy Spirit so we may obtain godly wisdom for instruction and correction.

Let's dig a bit deeper into this seed sowing. But first, I'd like to take it back a bit and focus on the groundwork here . . . literally. In agriculture, if a farmer intends to produce a harvest of corn, they first have to prepare the ground to receive the seed. We call this cultivation. It involves turning the soil and placing certain nutrients into the ground to enrich the soil.

The owner of this field already knows the demographic of the soil; they know how it's affected by the seasons and what needs to be done to properly prepare the ground so it can receive and not reject the seed. Stay with me on this. God knows us to the inner core of our soul; he knows what makes us tick, our likes and dislikes, what drives us, what discourages us, and what makes us happy or sad. When He draws us to Himself, He already knows the lay of the land (the real us). He knows who He's dealing with so we can't outthink or attempt to get over on God. He is what we call omniscient, which means, all-knowing. It is God alone who prepares us; some need more tilling than others . . . ha! I'm speaking of myself here, of course.

As I stated earlier in this book. God wants us to come to Him as we are, no matter how broken. He isn't looking for our human perfection as it can't compare to the renewing that comes from Him. Remember, God restores us into our original place in him, which is "in His likeness." Well, you may say, "What if I don't want to be changed? What if I'm happy with the person I am today? I don't need God to change me." Well, my friend, I'd say you have a spirit of pride.

When your heart is surrendered to God, nothing is about you anymore. It's about honoring God. We submit ourselves to say, "Have your way in me, God. Do what you will. I trust you and know my life is in your hands." You alone know my end from my beginning, and you know what's best for me.

God isn't looking to turn your life upside down. He wants to turn it right side up! Ha! If you're reading this book, you realize that there is something within you that needs to be yielded to God. You want to be free! You no longer want to live a life of uncertainty or being in bondage to anxiety, worry, doubt, and fear!

Let God have His way in you today. How? Talk to Him. He is a great listener! Sit before Him in a private quite place, even if you have to go to your garage and sit in your car. My husband actually prays in our garage! It's a place where he can cry out, pray, and not be disturbed. I prefer my closet; although time to time, my Yorkipoo Rusty likes to barge in during prayer, but I personally think he's drawn to the anointing! Ha!

Back to my point, find a place where you can be still and free from distraction. Empty your thoughts and heart to God. Tell Him your fears and doubts. Be honest. After you release, then be still and allow the Holy Spirit to minister to you. Quiet your thoughts and just be available, and God will begin an inner working in you that is life-transforming. Sometimes it subtle and sometimes dramatic! Just allow God to be God and do what He does best.

After the soil has been cultivated, the ground is ready to receive seed. The seed is the Bread of Life, God's Word, which is alive! You get this Word inside you and watch God produce a harvest in you that will make you look in the mirror and say, "I love this new me!"

Hebrews 4:12 (AMPC) tells us, "For the Word that God speaks is alive and full of power [making it active, operative, energizing, and effective]; it is sharper than any two-edged sword, penetrating to the dividing line of the breath of life (soul) and [the immortal] spirit, and of joints and marrow [of the deepest parts of our nature], exposing and sifting and analyzing and judging the very thoughts and purposes of the heart."

I want you to understand that the Word of God lives in the spirit realm.

John 4:24 (KJV) tells us, "God is a Spirit: and they that worship him must worship him in spirit and in truth."

When spoken in the earth realm it is activated in *full power!*

Luke 11:2 (AMPC) states, "And He said to them, when you pray, say: Our Father Who is in heaven, hallowed be Your name, Your kingdom come. *Your will be done* [held holy and revered] *on earth as it is in heaven"* (emphasis mine).

This is our blueprint for prayer. When we speak God's Word, which is His will in heaven, it is released to be established in the earth. When we listen to or read Scripture, it is released as a seed into us and planted by the Holy Spirit Himself. When we pray, expect an answer, expect revelation, and expect to see your petition granted!

Back to our agriculture expression. Jeremiah 17:8 (ESV) tells us, "He is like a tree planted by water, that sends out its roots by the stream, and does not fear when heat comes, for its leaves remain green, and is not anxious in the year of drought, for it does not cease to bear fruit."

Who is Jeremiah referring to in this scripture? God's Word is speaking about you! God's Word is often referred to as "Living Water" because we are planted in Him and receive our nourishment from this life-giving water; we are always increasing! Trying times will come in form of dry or wilderness seasons, but our outer experiences cannot and will not affect, delay, or stop what God has put in us from continually and consistently producing in our lives.

How does all of this connect to me identifying my why? We need to establish God's will as the primary and most essential factor in our lives. Nothing else takes precedence. When you have arrive to the place in your believer's walk where life is not about the money, success, or things but being in the center of God's will through every season of our lives, then you have found your why!

What drives me to press through every season of my life and not give up? My heart's desire is God. Whatever pleases Him, I want to do it! Nothing comes before God in my life. I don't need to be concerned about anything else because God is concerned about me.

Remember, 1 Peter 5:7 (ESV) tells us, "Casting all your anxieties on him, because he cares for you." He ensures I have everything I need plus benefits, ha! I never have lack in any area of my life. God is in charge of my relationships, marriage, children, businesses, ministries, finances, properties . . . everything! God provides my husband and me with the wisdom to maintain what He has placed under our care and authority. This, my friend, is how you can be set free from worry, fear, doubt, anxiety, and any of its demonic cousins!

You may ask, "Why then do I see Christians going through things? If God is a provider, why are people still poor or suffering from different areas in their lives?"

God's Word doesn't say that we won't encounter trouble or suffer afflictions. In fact, Romans 8:35–39 (AMPC) tells us:

> Who shall ever separate us from Christ's love? Shall suffering and affliction and tribulation? Or calamity and distress? Or persecution or hunger or destitution or peril or sword? Even as it is written, For Thy sake we are put to death all the day long; we are regarded and counted as sheep for the slaughter. Yet amid all these things we are more than conquerors and gain a surpassing victory through Him Who loved us. For I am persuaded beyond doubt (am sure) that neither death nor life, nor angels nor principalities, nor things impending and threatening nor things to come, nor powers, nor height nor depth, nor anything else in all creation will be able to separate us from the love of God which is in Christ Jesus our Lord.

So, you see, there are afflictions and tribulations that we will face as Christians. Heck, you are guaranteed to face these things apart from God! But wouldn't you rather go through the challenges with God on your side? The Scripture said that NOTHING will separate you from God's love! This is a promise to the believer. We go through, yes, but we go through with God! He provides everything we need by equipping us for the battles ahead. How?

Psalm 34:17–20 (ESV) says, "When the righteous cry for help, the Lord hears and delivers them out of all their troubles. The Lord is near to the brokenhearted and saves the crushed in spirit. Many are the afflictions of the righteous, but the Lord delivers him out of them all. He keeps all his bones; not one of them is broken."

In addition, John 14:1 (AMPC) tells us, "Do not let your hearts be troubled (distressed, agitated). You believe in and adhere to and trust in and rely on God; believe in and adhere to and trust in and rely also on Me."

My friend, life happens, but God will see to it that we make it through victoriously! We won't look like the hell we've been through because God covered us!

But why does He allow afflictions and tribulations?

Romans 5:1–5 (AMPC) tells us:

Therefore, since we are justified (acquitted, declared righteous, and given a right standing with God) through faith, let us [grasp the fact that we] have [the peace of reconciliation to hold and to [enjoy] peace with God through our Lord Jesus Christ (the Messiah, the Anointed One). Through Him also we have [our] access (entrance, introduction) by faith into this grace (state of God's favor) in which we [firmly and safely] stand. And let us rejoice and exult in our hope of experiencing and enjoying the glory of God. Moreover [let us also be full of joy now!] let us exult and triumph in our troubles and rejoice in our sufferings, knowing that ***pressure and affliction** and hardship **produce patient** and **unswerving endurance**. And **endurance** (fortitude) develops **maturity*** *of character (approved faith and tried integrity)*. And **char-acter** *[of this sort] produces [the habit of] joyful and* **confident hope** *of eternal salvation*. Such hope never disappoints or deludes or shames us, for God's love has been poured out in our hearts through the Holy Spirit Who has been given to us" (emphasis mine).

BAM! This Scripture seals and settles it!

# LET'S GO GET IT!

If you desire a strong intimate relationship with God, then expect to go through things! He has to build godly character within us. The only way to rid ourselves of our former ways and thoughts and character is to allow God to take you through challenges. This is where we are made! Because we are surrendered and in the center of God's will for our lives, He is bringing His best out in us. The tests aren't designed to kill us but make us strong in Him! satan wants to kill you for sure, but God protects us from every scheme and trap. It will never prevail!

You may have been in the enemy's grasp for some time now, battling against depression, anxiety, and separation. I tell you today that you can escape from beneath the footstool of satan! You no longer have to bend your back to the enemy! If you follow the basic fundamentals I've provided in this book, you can reverse the hold and place the enemy under your feet!

I dare you to declare today, "I am no longer bound to worry! I am no longer bound to fear! I am no longer bound to anxiety! I am no longer bound to doubt! The Greater One who lives inside me reigns in my life from this day forward! I know my why, and I will not be swayed nor shaken from my position and purpose in God! God chose me, God loves me, and if God is for me, who can against me! I press forward in the victory I have over satan's agents sent to deter me! No longer will I give place to satan in my life! Today I die to my former self and live under the redemptive resurrection power of Jesus!"

The blessings and promises of God in His Word belong to me! My ministry shall prosper! My businesses shall prosper! My marriage is fruitful! My children are saved and will honor the statues of God all their lives! My household is blessed and highly favored of the Lord! Everyone connected to me is blessed because the roots of my blessings run deep! Nothing can stop me! My aim is limitless because my God has no limits!

I vow to God this day to study His Word so that I may show myself approved! I am of the royal priesthood! I am an ambassador of Christ Jesus! I am a representative of the kingdom of heaven! I place my hope and trust in the Lord in every area of my life! I operate in the authority given me to have dominion in the earth, and I will call those things that are not as though they are! I speak into my destiny, I speak into the lives of my children, and I speak into the atmosphere of my community! There will be no lack. I come against spirits of antichrist that are sent to destroy households! I will leave a legacy and inheritance for the generations that will come after me!

Today and the rest of my natural life, I am living my very best blessed life!

# WORK CITED

[1] "Purpose", definition, Webster 1828 Dictionary https://www.webstersdictionary1828.com/purpose, v4.2022.7.2.3. MLA Accessed10 Oct 2022

[2] "Process." Merriam-Webster.com Dictionary, Merriam-Webster, https://www.merriam-webster.com/dictionary/process. MLA Accessed 11 Oct. 2022.

CPSIA information can be obtained
at www.ICGtesting.com
Printed in the USA
BVHW091056090223
658201BV00015B/784

9 781662 863806